100 LEO'S
Wit & Wisdom from Leo Burnett

LEO BURNETT COMPANY, INC.

NTC Business Books
a division of *NTC Publishing Group* • Lincolnwood, Illinois USA

Published by NTC Business Books, a division of NTC Publishing Group
4255 West Touhy Avenue
Lincolnwood, (Chicago) Illinois, 60646-1975, U.S.A.
Telephone: 708 679 5500

5 6 7 8 9 DP 9 8 7 6 5 4 3 2 1

CONTENTS

INTRODUCTION

Born October 21, 1891, in St. Johns, Michigan, Leo Burnett gained his first exposure to advertising layout and copy at his father's dry goods store. In 1914, he graduated from the University of Michigan with a degree in journalism and landed a job earning $18 a week as a reporter at the *Peoria (Ill.) Journal.*

Burnett went on to become advertising manager for the Detroit-based Cadillac Motor Company and creative head at the Homer McKee

Company, Indianapolis' leading ad agency, before moving to Chicago and assuming the position of creative vice president for Erwin Wasey advertising agency.

Borrowing against his life insurance policy, mortgaging his home, and scraping together "every cent and pants button" he could find, on August 5, 1935, the 44-year-old entrepreneur founded Leo Burnett Company, Inc., the first office being a suite in Chicago's Palmer House hotel.

With the firm belief that "the work of an advertising agency is warmly and immediately human and deals with human needs, wants, dreams and hopes," Burnett set out to create that kind of advertising. And did. Working hard and long hours—often beginning his days at 5 a.m.—his capacity for endless labor inspired those whom he employed.

"Leo had that ability, like a good athletic coach has, of making you do better than you thought you could," recalled his wife, Naomi. "In pleasing him, you were pleased with yourself. He somehow improved everything he touched, with either his black pencil or by his example. He had infinite patience."

Through 36 years under its spirited founder—the last four of which he assumed the title of founder chairman—the Leo Burnett Company created some of history's most enduring advertising campaigns, ranging from the Marlboro Cowboy to Kellogg's Tony the Tiger to the "Friendly Skies" of United Airlines to the Jolly Green Giant, among others. Although Burnett died in 1971, his original corporate mission to "Create the best advertising in the world—bar none" today continues to motivate more than 6,400 intensely loyal Burnetters in more than 60 offices worldwide.

THE
APPLE STORY

Apples have been saying "welcome" to Leo Burnett Company visitors since August 5,1935. On that hot day in the middle of the Depression, supreme optimist Leo Burnett and eight associates opened the doors of their newly formed advertising agency for the first time. To brighten up the place, the receptionist set out a bowl of apples.

When word got around Chicago that Leo Burnett was serving apples to his visitors, a newspaper columnist cracked, "It won't be long 'til Leo Burnett is *selling* apples on the street corner instead of giving them away." To be fair, the columnist was only echoing what seemed obvious to everyone but Leo Burnett and his band of believers: that it was the height of folly to start an advertising agency in the midst of the Depression.

But what the naysayers didn't understand was Leo's unique blend of vision and logic: "When you're on your economic bottom, then the *only* way to go is up." Leo was right. From those beginnings, when the entire staff could sit comfortably around a card table, and three accounts made up the client list, the Leo Burnett Company has grown into one of the world's largest agencies, billing more than $4.5 billion each year.

Representing the spirit of caring and concern for employees and clients alike, the apples have been on reception desks in Burnett offices every day. The agency still offers them to every visitor, and employees as well. In the last ten years, the Chicago headquarters alone gave away more than 3 million of them. Currently it gives away more than 1,500 each working day. Burnett offices around the world also follow the apple tradition, giving visitors and employees ample food for thought.

100 LEO'S

1
LEO

"When you reach for the stars
you may not quite get one,
but you won't come up with a
handful of mud either."

"To swear off making mistakes is very easy. All you have to do is swear off having ideas."

3
LEO

"Loss of humility can wreck our judgment. Smug complacency can put a roadblock in front of our progress."

"There is no such thing as a permanent advertising success."

"Personal satisfaction, I believe, must come in a day-to-day feeling that one has earned his or her pay."

"Rarely have I seen any really great advertising created without a certain amount of confusion, throw-aways, bent noses, irritation and downright cursedness."

7
LEO

"Fun without sell gets nowhere but sell without fun tends to become obnoxious."

"The sole purpose of business is
service. The sole purpose of advertising
is explaining the service which
business renders."

"One thing this company has never been is stuffy. And this is a valuable thing not to have been and is very much a part of what makes us tick."

"Keep it simple. Let's do the obvious thing—the common thing—but let's do it uncommonly well."

11
LEO

"The most fearful possibility
that lies ahead is that we might contract
'fatheadism'—fat between the ears
can destroy us."

12
LEO

"We want consumers to say,
'That's a hell of a product' instead of
'That's a hell of an ad.'"

13
LEO

"**P**lan the sale when you plan the ad."

14
LEO

"Regardless of the moral issue, dishonesty in advertising has proved very unprofitable."

15 LEO

"**I**f you can't turn yourself into your customer, you probably shouldn't be in the ad writing business at all."

"If you can't make a good ad in Chicago, you can't make one anywhere."

"The competent creative man does not approach his job solely in terms of making an advertisement, or a series of advertisements. He must approach it with a clear understanding of what other factors are involved in the sale of the product."

"In a world where nobody seems to know what's going to happen next, the only thing to do to keep from going completely nuts from frustration is plain old-fashioned work."

"Curiosity about life in all of its aspects, I think, is still the secret of great creative people."

"**O**ur real purpose in life is that
of improving the sales effectiveness
and reputation of our clients
through ideas."

21
LEO

"There is a paradise of improvement awaiting us if we search hard enough for it."

"I have learned that it pays to fight
for concepts and causes that may appear
unpopular at the moment, rather than
following the course of quick and easy
agreement."

"It is apparent that the company can't be any better or bigger than the growth of the people in it."

"In this agency business we are people talking to people, and that's what we should keep running through our fingers."

"Let's gear our advertising to sell our goods, but let's recognize also that advertising has a broad social responsibility."

"If you're not fertile and imaginative and full of wonder and curiosity, I urge you to stay away from advertising."

27
LEO

"'Too-bigness' has set in when the hot pursuit of profits cuts corners on old-fashioned ethics."

"A really good creative person is more interested in earnestness than in glibness and takes more satisfaction out of converting people than in 'wowing' them."

29
LEO

"Ideas alone enable a man to survive and flourish."

"When a man knows deep in his bones what is right, and keeps acting on it, he avoids the trap of compromise— he remains incorruptible."

"A company in which anyone is afraid to speak up, to differ, to be daring and original, is closing the coffin door on itself."

32
LEO

"Half the pleasure of getting big, I think, is to thumb your nose at the indignity of getting dignified."

**33
LEO**

"Let's continue to be known as an agency which spends more time trying to *improve* its theories rather than to *defend* them."

34
LEO

"Collective solutions to problems start with individual human beings and individual efforts."

"Growing pains sometimes may seem unbearable, but believe me they are nothing compared with the pain of shrinking or the pain of standing still."

"Advertising says to people, 'Here's what we've got. Here's what it will do for you. Here's how to get it.'"

"The work of an advertising agency is warmly and immediately human. It deals with human needs, wants, dreams and hopes. Its 'product' cannot be turned out on an assembly line."

"I have learned that any fool can write a bad ad, but that it takes a real genius to keep his hands off a good one."

**39
LEO**

"Good advertising does not just circulate information. It penetrates the public mind with desires and belief."

**40
LEO**

"The only creative conference worth a damn is one in which everybody in the room starts from the same base of fact, a consuming appetite for ideas no matter how wild they may first appear, and a humble respect for them."

41
LEO

"I have learned that you can't have
good advertising without a good client,
that you can't keep a good client without
good advertising, and no client will
ever buy better advertising than
he understands or has an appetite for."

"If you have the facts on your side
and honest conviction in your heart, you
rarely lose by fighting for your idea
all the way."

"Are you blowing opportunity after opportunity because you can't recognize a crossroad when you come to it?"

44 LEO

"**O**ur business is ideas. They grow and flourish best in an atmosphere of congenial collaboration."

45
LEO

"It seems to us there should be
less concern about the dimensions of a
business. And considerably more
concern about its heartbeat—the values,
zest and spirit behind its physical and
financial facade."

"In looking for creative people,
I am always most interested in those
who have an almost naive curiosity
about life."

47
LEO

"The greatest thing to be achieved
in advertising, in my opinion,
is believability, and nothing is more
believable than the product itself."

"Before you can have a share
of market, you must have a share
of mind."

49
LEO

"The public does not know what it wants, and there is no sure way of finding out until the idea is exposed under normal conditions of sale. If people could tell you in advance what they want, there would never have been a wheel, a lever, much less an automobile, an airplane or a TV set."

"A good ad which is not run never produces sales."

51
LEO

"Too many ads that try not to go over the reader's head end up beneath his notice."

52
LEO

<hr>

"I have learned that it is far easier
to write a speech about good advertising
than it is to write a good ad.**"**

"In all of our planning I like to feel that we adventurously live on the fringe of the Great Creative Unknown, but if we are properly armed with facts we are always better prepared to enter it."

"In my opinion, there has been only one indispensable man in the history of the world. His name was Adam."

"I like to look on our own shop as kind of a barefoot agency which is mentally always trying to put itself into other people's shoes—a working ranch rather than a dude ranch."

"We built our business not so much by *getting* accounts as *building* them."

"As I have observed it, great advertising writing, either in print or TV, is always deceptively and disarmingly simple. It has the common touch without being or sounding patronizing."

"I am one who believes that one of the greatest dangers of advertising is not that of misleading people, but that of boring them to death."

59
LEO

"The secret of all effective originality in advertising is not the creation of new and tricky words and pictures, but one of putting familiar words and pictures into new relationships."

60
LEO

"In this business when you start putting the emphasis on counting money rather than getting out better ads and otherwise giving your clients better service, you soon learn that there is very little money to count."

**61
LEO**

―――――――――――

"The greatest saving of all is better utilization of our time. This directly affects practically every phase of the business in terms of expense and profits."

"I have always taken the attitude that
no account is a 'problem account'
but that all accounts have important
problems attached to them—
that you can waste more time and burn
up more nervous energy by fighting
a problem than by taking a positive
attitude and solving it."

"In learning to work and live with people, the
most important thing I am coming to understand
is the simple truth that 'no one makes mistakes
on purpose.' Knowing this should allow us to
concentrate on correcting the mistake rather than
making life miserable for the mistake maker.
If he is the right sort, nothing you can say or do
to him will make him feel any worse about the
mistake than he does already."

64
LEO

"Agencies that create great
advertising may become big agencies,
but their goal remains the creation
of great advertising."

"Make it simple. Make it
memorable. Make it inviting to look at.
Make it fun to read."

"Creative ideas flourish best in a shop which preserves some spirit of fun. Nobody is in business for fun, but that does not mean there cannot be fun in business."

"In operating a business of our size, it is obvious that we have to be well departmentalized. This does not mean, however, that we have to be *channelized*."

"The biggest problem of all, as I see it, is a human one—how to keep from *acting* big."

"'Reaching for the Stars' may sound a little naive, but it is a thought in which I passionately believe; and maybe the world could use a little more naiveté of that kind."

"It is this spirit (Reaching for the Stars) which I think has made many of us work long hours, which makes us carry the thought of our work with us wherever we go, which makes us lay aside good work for better work."

71
LEO

"**I** have always felt that advertising
could be something to get excited about.
To take pleasure in. To regard as
worthwhile, meaningful, respectable.
Something to do thoughtfully
and well."

"Anyone who thinks that people can be fooled or pushed around has an inaccurate and pretty low estimate of people—and he won't do very well in advertising."

"**I** listen to everybody and take notes. Particularly salesmen. They get close to people."

"It's important in building our organizational machines not to exclude the dissenter, the 'Outsider,' the non-conformist."

"It seems axiomatic that you have to make a friend before you can effectively make him a proposition."

"If you are writing about baloney,
don't try to make it Cornish hen, because
that is the worst kind of baloney there is.
Just make it darned good baloney."

"The grist for our mill is still words.
Words as they put the sock and soul into
the expression of ideas."

"Take a firm stand against
putting expediency above principle;
bluff ahead of facts."

"A good basic selling idea,
involvement and relevancy, of course,
are as important as ever, but in the
advertising din of today, unless
you make yourself noticed and believed,
you ain't got nothin.'"

80
LEO

"These things pay off—good taste, a high standard of ethics, an attitude of public responsibility and low pressure."

"**M**y only warning is that growth never compromises integrity, and I regard integrity as the heart and driving force of this agency."

"I have learned to practice
what I call
'constructive dissatisfaction.'"

83
LEO

"I regard a great ad
as the most beautiful thing
in the world."

"A real idea has a
power of its own and a life
of its own."

85
LEO

"Cling like wildcats to the only realities we can swear we have hold of— our own sacred and individual integrities."

86
LEO

"Steep yourself in your subject, work like hell, and love, honor and obey your hunches."

"Whatever success I have enjoyed, I attribute almost entirely to a deep personal sense of responsibility to our clients and to the job at hand, with a passion for thoroughness, often at considerable personal sacrifice, and an unyielding intolerance of sloppy thinking, sloppy work and almost-good-enough jobs."

"Good advertising is a happy wedding of words and pictures, not a contest between them."

89
LEO

"I believe that superior creative work always has been, is, and always will be the hub of the wheel in any successful agency."

"I look for craftsmen in words and pictures who so completely understand good creative masonry and are so skilled in it, that when they lay a brick out of place they do it on purpose."

"
. . . In its performance, advertising is not a soloist. It is a member of an ensemble of all those activities that can be classified under the general head of marketing, and it must do its part in harmony with them if the end result is to be good."

"The only sound basis of a personal service relationship is mutual confidence and respect. Unless that exists at the start, the account will eventually represent loss and disappointment."

"Friction makes sparks
and sparks start great creative
conflagrations."

"Promises must be kept, deadlines met, commitments honored; not just for the sake of old-fashioned morality, but because we become what we do (or fail to do), and character is simply the sum of our performances."

"Advertising cannot perform magic for an unwanted or undesirable product. But a skilled advertising man can present previously overlooked virtues in a product in a way that will make people reach for it."

"**P**lan ahead but maintain flexibility."

97
LEO

"We should constantly remind ourselves that the most productive use of our own time offers the greatest opportunity for increased income for us as individuals and for better earnings for our company."

"This is as good a time as any to start examining ourselves for any of those tell-tale signs of success that lead to inner rot. Those signs are complacency. . . coasting. . . bureaucracy."

"You can grow up in the advertising business, but you don't have to grow old in it."

**100
LEO**

"**I** am often asked how I
got into this business. I didn't.
The business got into me."

WHEN TO TAKE
MY NAME
OFF THE DOOR

Somewhere along the line, after I'm finally off the premises, you or your successors may want to take my *name* off the premises, too.

You may want to call yourselves "Twain, Rogers, Sawyer and Finn, Inc.". . . Or "Ajax Advertising". . . or Something.

That will certainly he okay with me if it's good for you.

But let me tell you when I might *demand* that you take my name off the door.

That will be the day when you spend more time trying to make money and *less* time making advertising—our kind of advertising.

When you forget that the sheer fun of ad-making and the lift you get out of it—the creative climate of the place—should be as important as money to the very special breed of writers and artists and business professionals who compose this company of ours—and make it tick.

When you lose that restless feeling that nothing you do is ever quite good enough.

When you lose your itch to do the job well for its own sake—regardless of the client, or the money, or the effort it takes.

When you lose your passion for thoroughness . . . your hatred of loose ends.

When you stop reaching for the manner, the overtones, the marriage of words and pictures that produces the fresh, the memorable, and the believable effect.

When you stop rededicating yourselves every

day to the idea that better advertising is what the Leo Burnett Company is all about.

When you are no longer what Thoreau called "a corporation with a conscience"—which means to me, a corporation of conscientious men and women.

When you begin to compromise your integrity —which has always been the heart's blood—the very guts of this agency.

When you stoop to convenient expediency and rationalize yourselves into acts of opportunism—for the sake of a fast buck.

When you show the slightest sign of crudeness, inappropriateness or smart-aleckness—and you lose that subtle sense of the fitness of things.

When your main interest becomes a matter of *size* just to be big—rather than good, hard, wonderful work.

When your outlook narrows down to the number of windows—from zero to five—in the walls of your office.

When you lose your humility and become big-shot weisenheimers. . . a little too big for your boots.

When the apples come down to being just apples for eating (or for polishing)—no longer a part of our tone—our personality.

When you disapprove of something, and start tearing the hell out of the *man who did it* rather than the work itself.

When you stop building on strong and vital *ideas,* and start a routine production line.

When you start believing that, in the interest of efficiency, a creative spirit and the urge to create can be delegated and administered, and forget that they can only be nurtured, stimulated, and inspired.

When you start giving lip service to this being a "creative agency" and stop really being one.

Finally, when you lose your respect for the *lonely man*—the man at his typewriter or his drawing board or behind his camera or just scribbling notes with one of our big black pencils—or working all night on a media plan. When you forget that the lonely man—and thank God for *him*—has made the agency we now have—possible. When you forget he's the man who, because he is reaching harder, sometimes actually gets hold of—for a moment—one of those hot, unreachable stars.

THAT, boys and girls, is when I shall *insist* you take my name off the door.

And by golly, it *will* be taken off the door.

Even if I have to materialize long enough some night to rub it out myself—on every one of your floors.

And before I DE-materialize again, I will paint out that star-reaching symbol, too.

And burn all the stationery.

Perhaps tear up a few ads in passing.

And throw every goddamned apple down the elevator shafts.

You just won't know the place, the next morning.

You'll *have* to find another name.

Leo Burnett

*All proceeds from the sale of this book
will be donated to the Advertising Council,
a not-for-profit organization
founded in 1942, of which Leo Burnett
was a charter member.*